Map of Route

Berg

W9-ANT-570

East Germany

West Germany

Peter, Andreas, Petra, and Günter Wetzel shortly after their escape from East Germany, enjoying their new life in West Germany.

"Wir (meine Familie und ich) sind froh darüber, dass wir uns damals dafür entschieden hatten, die Flucht zu wagen und die DDR zu verlassen. Wir haben diese Flucht auch innerhalb der zurückliegenden 35 Jahre niemals bereut."

"We (my family and I) are glad that we decided back then to risk the escape and leave the GDR. Since then, for the past 35 years, we have never regretted our escape."

—Günter Wetzel

To my mom, who got to read my story but never saw it in print.

Special thanks to Günter Wetzel and his family for sharing their story, to the Anderson Abruzzo International Balloon Museum in New Mexico and the National Balloon Museum in Iowa for answering questions on balloon science and history, and to Museum Naila in Germany where the original balloon is exhibited.

And finally, to my fabulous husband, Rusty; awesome agent, Kendra; and extraordinary editor, REL.

—KF

Flight for Freedom

The Wetzel Family's Daring Escape from East Germany

By Kristen Fulton

Illustrated by Torben Kuhlmann

chronicle books·san francisco

In the days when Germany was divided by a wall,
life was very different.

For nearly nine hundred miles, concrete and steel sliced through the country.

On the west side, children watched cartoons, wore blue jeans, and ate pizza.

In the East, children watched the news, wore scratchy uniforms, and waited in long lines for a banana once a year.

Six-year-old Peter Wetzel understood the difference.
He lived on the wrong side, the east side.

Every night at nine o'clock the lights
went out in every house in East Germany.
It was the law.

But tonight a small candle danced, throwing shadows against a picture torn from a West German newspaper. Peter's hands shook as he looked at the image of people in a hot-air balloon.

He knew why his mama and papa had kept it hidden under their mattress—that picture was illegal. Peter also knew that it was part of Mama and Papa's secret plan.

As the wind whistled outside the window on a cold night in 1978, Peter's life was about to change forever.

Peter watched as his family sat around the table with their best friends, the Strelzyks, and hatched a plan. He listened as his papa and mama discussed what they needed: almost two hundred yards of fabric. Heavy-duty thread. Fuel. And scrap metal, to make a basket large enough to hold both families.

They had to succeed.

Even if they all kept their secret, this escape wouldn't be easy.
The government noticed everything.

Month after month, Mama purchased only a few yards of nylon fabric at a time.

Week after week, Papa purchased just a couple of gallons of fuel at a time.

Day after day, Peter walked to school in his starched uniform. He passed soldiers carrying rifles and big dogs that barked and growled.

Every night for more than a year, Peter lay on his bed watching the light from Papa's welding flicker underneath his bedroom door.

His eyes fluttered closed as he was lulled to sleep by the *put-a-put-a-put* of the sewing machine up in the attic.

Each morning when Peter woke, he expected to find proof that his parents were building a balloon. But, the house was exactly as it had been the day before.

Everything hidden.

Everything quiet.

Peter wondered if the photo had been only a dream.
Would he ever escape East Germany? Have a sleepover? Not be afraid?
He wanted to ask his mama and papa, but they had made him promise
never to talk about the picture.

Hard as it was, Peter kept his promise.

Just past midnight on September 16, 1979, Peter's parents gently shook him awake.

It was time.

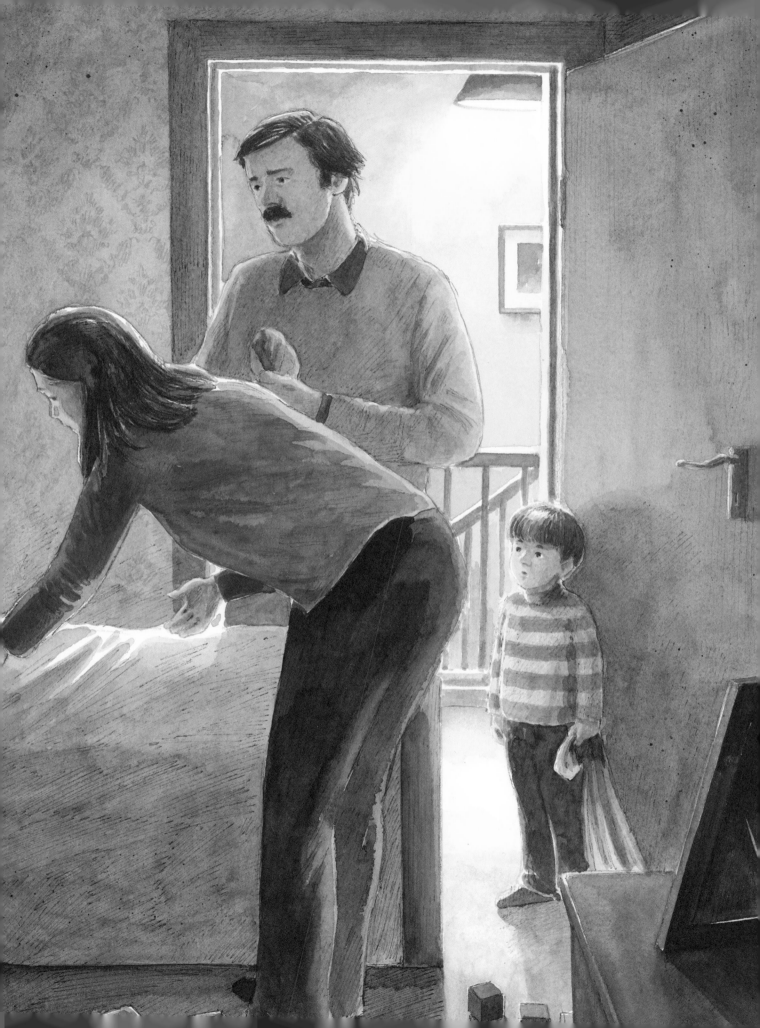

They tiptoed outside, each bringing one small knapsack.

Piling into their car, they tried to close the doors softly.
But like a clap of thunder, the sharp clicks echoed
through the calm night.

As the car crept forward, Peter stared backward
and whispered goodbye.

The weather was perfect. The thick clouds would help hide them. With luck, the wind would blow them toward the West, to freedom.

They stopped the car in a huge field surrounded by a thick cluster of trees. Peter helped to unload the balloon, gas tanks, and giant blowtorch. He held a side of the balloon, while the others used the blowtorch to heat the air.

Peter watched as the warm air slowly stretched the fabric to look more like a balloon.

Would this bundle of mismatched fabric even make
it over the wall?

A siren wailed in the distance.
The Stasi!

Peter's heart pounded. How did the police find out?
He had kept his promise. He hadn't told a soul.
Someone must have tattled on them.

Peter's fingers gripped the nylon fabric tighter as the last puff of air inflated the balloon. Billowing off the ground, the balloon stood taller than the trees. Trembling with fear and excitement, they all scurried into the basket.

Papa handed a knife to Peter and told him to cut the rope, their last tie to East Germany. The knife trembled in Peter's hand. The barking guard dogs were getting closer.

Peter sawed back and forth against the tightly woven rope, bit by bit, shred by shred— breaking through the rope and breaking free.

The balloon climbed.

Higher! Higher! They had to get higher.
Peter watched as the needle on the meter moved.

Two thousand feet.
Guards spilled into the forest
where they had just been.

One thousand feet.
A distant spotlight broke the night.

Three thousand feet.

The balloon began to tear.

Four thousand feet.

Two of their six gas tanks were empty.

Five thousand feet.

Four empty gas tanks.

Six thousand feet.

The last tank of gas sputtered.
The balloon descended——too fast!

The balloon fell faster and faster. Peter's stomach churned and turned.
They had only been in the air for thirty minutes. Papa didn't think they
had gone far enough to cross the wall. If they hadn't, he knew they would
be seized, separated, and sent to prison.

Peter cried as they plummeted.

They crashed to the ground in a thicket of trees.

Lights beamed in the distance, heading in their direction.
Peter feared they were caught.

Scrambling behind trees, they stifled their voices,
sweating even in the cold.

The lights washed over their hiding place . . .
and zoomed right past them.
It was only a car.
But Peter had never seen a car that looked like
that. Papa's voice quivered as he explained that
wasn't just any car. That was a West German car.
They did it! They actually did it!

Emerging from the trees one by one, they walked toward town. The night passed in slow motion. Each step carried them farther away from the nine hundred miles of concrete and steel.

Papa pulled a surprise from his knapsack.
With a spark and a toss, firecrackers exploded
across the West German sky.
And Peter and his family celebrated.

THE BALLOON

Constructing the Balloon: On her annual visit, in January 1978, Petra Wetzel's sister smuggled a section from a West German newspaper to the Wetzel family by hiding it under her dress. It featured a photo of the Albuquerque International Balloon Fiesta in New Mexico. At the time, this photo was all the Wetzel and Strelzyk families knew about hot-air balloons, and it was the inspiration for their escape. The Wetzel and Strelzyk families used their knowledge of physics and mathematics to create a working balloon, from calculating factors such as balloon size and temperature to sourcing effective materials. These technical details were essential to a viable escape plan.

Size: The calculations used to design the final, successful balloon were based on a homemade pattern (seen on facing page). The balloon was designed to be much larger than an average hot-air balloon—it was approximately 60 feet (18 metres) in diameter and 90 feet (27 metres) high—in part because of the number of people it needed to carry and the height it had to achieve to clear the wall and reach their destination. Some sources speculate their balloon may have traveled as high as 8,000 feet (2,438 metres) based on their trajectory, but since their equipment gave out at 6,000 feet (1,829 metres), we can't be sure.

Balloon Materials: This colorful balloon (see photo) is the actual balloon the Wetzel and Strelzyk families flew in their final escape, reinflated here for promotional material for the film *The Night Crossing*. Note the wide variety of fabric used! After testing the porosity of several fabrics using a vacuum cleaner hose, among other materials found at home, they settled on nylon—a sturdy, lightweight material that also has a high melting temperature. Because acquiring large quantities of nylon was both challenging and dangerous (as it could be seen as suspicious by East German authorities), they also used other fabrics such as bedsheets and shower lining.

Reinflated for promotional purposes, this is the actual balloon used to escape.

Gondola Materials: Here Peter (age seven) and Andreas (age three) Wetzel pose in the balloon's basket, often called the "gondola" of a balloon, shortly after their successful escape. This gondola was less than 5 feet by 5 feet (1.5 metres by 1.5 metres), and held all eight members of the Wetzel and Strelzyk families as they soared more than 6,000 feet (1,829 metres) above the ground. The base was welded scrap steel, with steel bars in each of the corners where the balloon could attach, and washing lines to serve as guardrails.

Peter and Andreas Wetzel pose on the gondola shortly after the escape.

Temperature: The bright tanks inside the gondola are tanks of propane gas that were attached to a burner and used to heat the air within the balloon itself, called an "envelope." The heated air inside the envelope is less dense than the cool air outside, causing the balloon to rise because it is lighter than the surrounding air. For their escape, the Wetzels and Strelzyks calculated that they needed to maintain at least a 176-degree Fahrenheit (80-degree Celsius) difference in temperature between the balloon envelope and the cold night air to carry all of them high enough and far enough. Heat makes a hot-air balloon rise, and venting—the process of allowing cool air into the envelope—makes it descend. As their gas tanks were used up, the temperature in the balloon cooled down, and they plummeted to the ground.

The gondola.

The uninflated balloon.

The inflated balloon.

ESCAPE ATTEMPTS

The Wetzel and Strelzyk families made three hot-air balloons, the third and final of which was the balloon that successfully transported them over the wall. The first balloon was made of a canvas-like fabric. During a trial run they discovered that the fabric did not allow moisture to wick away. Instead, the weight of the condensation gathered on the top of the balloon and caused the fabric to collapse onto the boiler. The second balloon had just as many issues, primarily with the boiler itself. As a result, the Wetzel family became concerned with safety and decided to find another way to escape, handing the finished second balloon over to the Strelzyks.

But, events conspired to change their plans. During the first escape, the families had inadvertently left a few tools behind. The families weren't initially worried that the discovery would endanger them since they were everyday items, and the Stasi, or East German Police, didn't know they had been used in an escape attempt. But, during the Strelzyks' second escape attempt—this time without the Wetzels—they had to flee, leaving the entire second balloon in a field near where the tools were discovered. The Stasi realized that both the balloon and the tools were being used in an escape attempt. The Stasi placed ads in the newspaper calling for information, and the Wetzel family knew it was only a matter of time before they were discovered. They had no choice. They had to escape, and they had to do it now. Their quickest option was to construct a third and final balloon.

The Wetzels and Strelzyks constructed that third, successful balloon in less than six weeks, and in the early morning of September 16, 1979, they finally made their harrowing escape. It took the balloon less than half an hour to go a little more than 15 miles (about 24 kilometres)—15 miles that changed their lives forever.

Günter Wetzel went on to become a pilot of small planes and a flight instructor, successfully returning to East Germany to help others escape across the wall. Günter, Petra, Peter, and Andreas Wetzel still live in Germany.

AUTHOR'S NOTE

After reading a small paragraph in a 1979 copy of *Time* magazine, I found myself in awe of the Wetzel family. Their perseverance to give their children the best life possible touched my heart. I found several articles in newspapers that told of their harrowing flight. But, I wanted more. I wanted to speak to the Wetzel family personally.

I was happy to discover Günter Wetzel still living in Germany. After exchanging several emails with me over a period of months, he agreed to meet me. As I prepared for my interview, I wondered what this real-life hero would be like. He may not have a cape or mask, but he risked it all, saved two families, and gave millions hope. I found Günter Wetzel everything a hero should be: kind and generous.

I wondered why he had chosen to share his story now. It had been 34 years since his brave escape, and he was sharing his story with me, an unknown author. Why? He told me that, after the escape, many people wanted to interview him, but he didn't feel comfortable sharing his story then. His children were so young, and he and Petra worried about putting them in the spotlight. And he feared for the safety of friends still living in East Germany if he spoke.

A sign in Bavaria marking the site of the balloon landing.

His response was that of a man who did what he had to do in harsh times, not one motivated by fame and glory. When the wall came down, the world seemed to forget about heroes like Günter who had risked their lives so long before. That is, until now.

While in Germany, I was able to retrace the Wetzels' escape on that night so long ago. The barriers that made up the wall between East and West Germany were often only as wide as a street—easy for us to walk today, but at one time filled with armed guards, land mines, and steel fencing. There is a tree near the town of Naila in Bavaria, Germany, that bears a balloon sign, marking the thicket of trees where the balloon landed.

THE COLD WAR AND THE BERLIN WALL

After World War II, Germany was divided among the victorious Allied powers. After some disagreement, it was decided that the west side would be controlled by Britain, the United States, and France, while the east side, governed by the German Democratic Republic, would be controlled by the Soviet Union. Almost three million East Germans fled their homes, to avoid living under the control of the Soviet Union, before the 900-mile (1,448-kilometre) long inner German border wall (separating East and West Germany) and the Berlin Wall prevented others from doing so. Over time each portion of the wall has become known by different names, but many people—including the Wetzels and Strelzyks—referred to both the inner German border wall and the Berlin Wall as the Berlin Wall.

The inner German border wall was built in 1945, and the Berlin Wall was built in 1961, both during the time known as the Cold War, a term used to describe political hostilities that stopped short of open warfare. By the time the walls were completed, there were almost seventeen million people locked behind them. Life abruptly changed for East Germans. East Germans were no longer allowed to leave the country, so many families were divided, and East Germans who had worked in West Germany found themselves jobless. The wall gave the German Democratic Republic even more control over the land and money of its East German citizens. Because goods were regulated, all East Germans had the same possessions, from clothes to toys to food. Because improvements were limited due to scarcities, many homes did not have bathtubs or showers and some did not have toilets. Freedom of speech was restricted, with radio stations and television stations limited to channels supporting East Germany. Finally, there was a pervasive atmosphere of fear.

These conditions created a strong urge to escape, although few escape attempts were successful. Here are a few other successful escape attempts:

> A group of students spent months using spoons to dig an underground tunnel beneath the Berlin Wall to West Germany.

> Over the years, several people tried to make themselves into human slingshots and fling their way across the barriers between the two countries. Unfortunately, few survived.

> Some swam or floated the 28 miles (45 kilometres) in rough current to cross the Baltic Sea into West Germany.

On June 12, 1987, U.S. President Ronald Reagan challenged Soviet Union leader Mikhail Gorbachev to "tear down this wall." Russia, the United States, and many other countries came together for peace talks, uniting and forming an alliance. On November 9, 1989, the inner German border wall and the Berlin Wall came down, and Germany was once again united.

The events in this book are accurate to the best of anyone's ability to recall them given the passage of time and the intensity of that time period.

Text copyright © 2020 by Kristen Fulton. Illustrations copyright © 2020 by Torben Kuhlmann. All rights reserved. No part of this book may be reproduced in any form without written permission from the publisher.

Library of Congress Cataloging-in-Publication Data available.

ISBN 978-1-4521-4960-8

Manufactured in China.

Design by Amelia Mack.
Typeset in Miso.

10 9 8 7 6 5 4 3 2 1

Chronicle Books LLC
680 Second Street
San Francisco, California 94107

Chronicle Books—we see things differently.
Become part of our community at
www.chroniclekids.com.

Chronicle books and gifts are available at special quantity discounts to corporations, professional associations, literacy programs, and other organizations. For details and discount information, please contact our premiums department at corporatesales@chroniclebooks.com or at 1-800-759-0190.

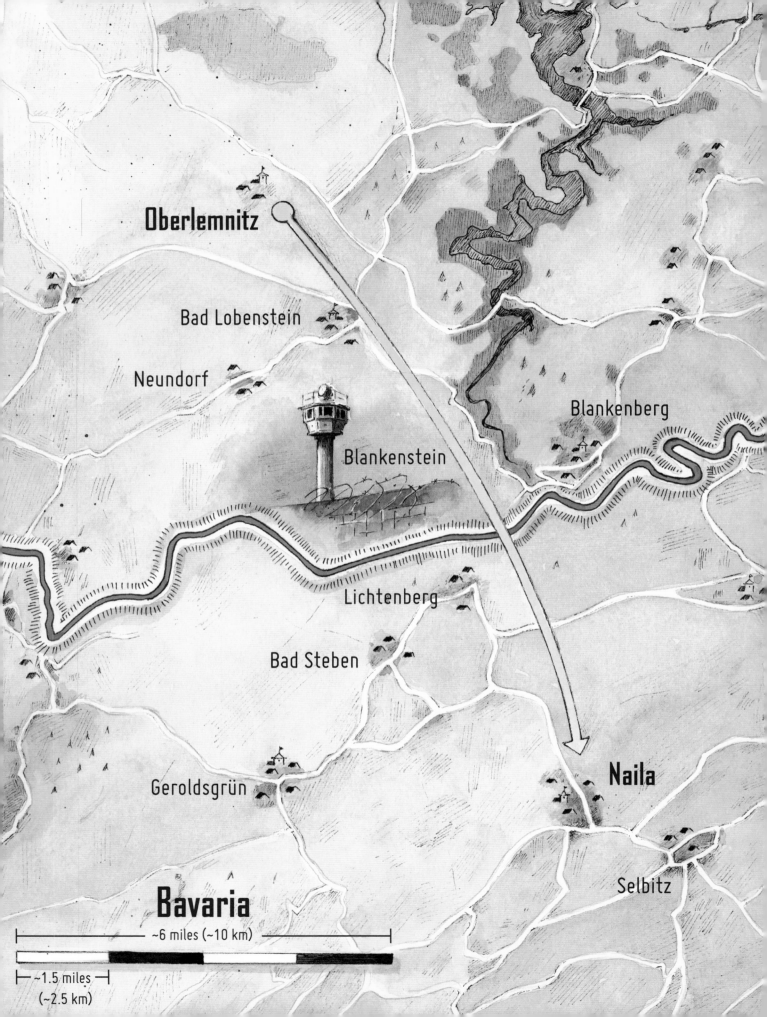

Oberlemnitz

Bad Lobenstein

Neundorf

Blankenstein

Blankenberg

Lichtenberg

Bad Steben

Geroldsgrün

Naila

Selbitz

Bavaria

~6 miles (~10 km)

~1.5 miles
(~2.5 km)

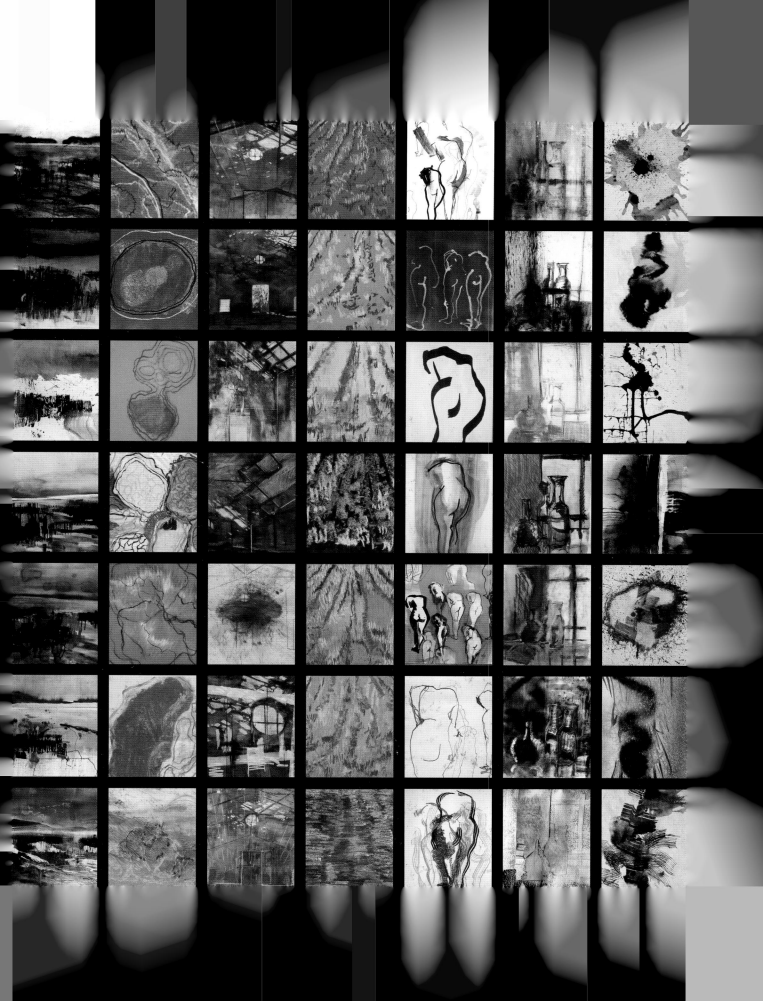